THE IMPORTANCE OF SELF-ASSESSMENT

Take control of your professional development

Written by Nicolas Zinque

Translated by Rebecca Neal

Coaching 50MINUTES.com

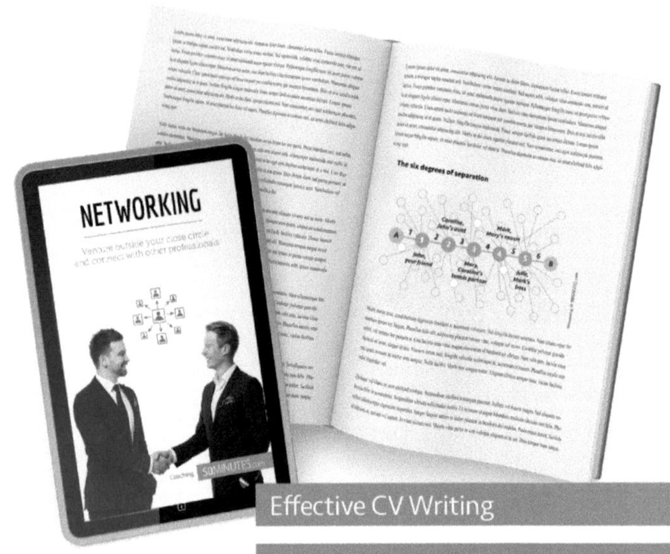

50MINUTES.com

PROPEL
YOUR BUSINESS FORWARD!

NETWORKING
Venture outside your close circle
and connect with other professionals

Coaching 50MINUTES.com

The six degrees of separation

Effective CV Writing

Resolving Office Conflict

Boost Your Concentration

Find Your Work-Life Balance

www.50minutes.com

HOW CAN
SELF-ASSESSMENT HELP ME?

- **Issue:** how can I develop an effective self-assessment programme in order to correctly evaluate my skills?
- **Uses:** realistically evaluating your strengths, weaknesses and overall performance allows you to improve and reach your goals more easily through self-knowledge.
- **Professional context:** skill development, management, career management, motivation, training, taking stock of your career.
- **FAQs:**
  - When should I assess myself?
  - How often should I plan self-assessment sessions?
  - What dangers am I likely to encounter when I assess myself?
  - What is the difference between an assessment grid and a self-assessment grid?
  - How can self-assessment help me to prepare for my yearly performance review?
  - What should I do if the results of my personal assessment are different from my yearly performance review?
  - Should I encourage my employees to assess themselves?

We are already familiar with assessment: it is inscribed in our culture, because from the time we first start school, we experience this frequently unpleasant process. And although we no longer receive good or bad grades in the professional world, we are nonetheless regularly appraised by our superiors. Although we sometimes dread and often criticise these evaluations, they are undeniably useful, particularly for judging our progress. However, assessment is much more complicated than it seems, and this is all the more true when we take on the double role of assessor and assessed! Indeed, when we are the only people responsible for the process, it is much easier to lose control of it.

Nonetheless, being able to evaluate oneself accurately is an indispensable skill in business. For employers, it is useful to hire an independent person who is capable of analysing their own work, successes and failures in order to progress. This self-assessment is, furthermore, obviously useful for the employee, as they are the main beneficiary of it! Self-assessment will help you to anticipate potential obstacles and achieve your goals more easily. In this way, the project that is so important to you, the crucial file that your boss has entrusted you with and your yearly performance review will be more likely to turn out well.

In 50 minutes, this guide will help you to create a persona-lised self-assessment grid in order to objectively measure your results, define your assets and areas for improvement in order to boost your productivity, and enable you to thrive professionally.

EFFECTIVE SELF-ASSESSMENT: THE BASICS

WHAT IS SELF-ASSESSMENT?

The process in brief

This concept comprises two words which, taken separately, can be easily understood:

- 'self';
- 'assessment'. According to the Collins English Dictionary, the verb 'assess' means "to judge the worth, importance, etc., of; evaluate".

Most of the time, we evaluate the people around us or they evaluate us. What is specific about self-assessment is that it involves an individual evaluating themselves. In theory, the only thing that changes is the target, but in practice this has major consequences. You may have already noticed that we do not treat ourselves in the same way that we treat others. Some people treat themselves leniently, even carelessly, whereas others are stricter with themselves than with others.

More than a sum of two words, self-assessment is a complex process which can be illustrated using the example of bodybuilding. In this sport, individuals develop their muscle mass for purely aesthetic purposes and then display their body during competitions. Although they practice in front of mirrors, this is not just to admire the result: it is also and above all to assess their work. Each person has their own physiology, which facilitates or hinders the muscle development of certain body parts. The bodybuilder must get to know their own body and their assets but, above all, their weaknesses. Indeed, although it is always more rewarding to work on their strong points, they must find a balance if they want a well-rounded physique. Based on an initial evaluation, they will develop an appropriate training programme in order to reach their goals. They will regularly have to adjust their exercises depending on their progress, and the only way they will be able to reach their goal is through these efforts.

This is self-assessment: getting to know yourself better, daring to look in the mirror and carrying out an objective appraisal by analysing your strengths and weaknesses in order to achieve your goal. It is important to devise a personalised assessment programme, because some individuals will learn certain skills more quickly than other people.

TIP

The comparison with the world of sports is not a coincidence. Indeed, even though great champions are surrounded by a team which includes their coach and physical and mental assistants, the main factors that have allowed them to reach the highest levels of their sport are their hard work, their discipline and their ability to evaluate themselves. During interviews, sportspeople often reveal tips and tricks regarding their mental state and their training methods. Take inspiration from them. Furthermore, if you lose sight of your goal, hold onto the image of bodybuilding: picture your project as the physique of a bodybuilder and identify which parts need to be improved.

In what context should it be used?

Self-assessment can prove useful in three different situations, based on the criteria 'before, during, after'.

- **'Before':** during our lives, we regularly have to take important decisions which may have major long-term consequences ("Shall I take the risk of quitting my stable job to realise my dream of starting my own business?"). Before embarking on a new adventure or a complicated project, it is essential to carry out an appraisal in order to weigh up the pros and cons and, above all, to understand the implications and issues at stake.
- **'During':** you may realise in the middle of a project that you are veering away from your initial aim or that the context has changed with the announcement of new technology, a change in the target of the new product, a reduction in the basic budget, etc. This is the time to evaluate the situation in order to adjust your methods for reaching your goal.
- **'After':** self-assessment of a project once it is complete is just as important for your subsequent work. Perhaps you want to know why a project that you spent several months on was so difficult to complete, or you have recently joined a company and are getting ready for your first performance review. Either way, an evaluation will

allow you to draw conclusions about the work you have carried out.

SELF-ASSESSMENT FOR EVERYBODY

Self-assessment is essential for personal projects that you are working on independently, because nobody will steer you back if you set off in the wrong direction. Nonetheless, this tool can be suitable for all types of jobs: if you are a subordinate in a big company, with no responsibility, there is nothing stopping you from assessing your work and trying to find ways to boost your effectiveness yourself. You will begin to thrive more in your day-to-day work and it is highly likely that your managers will recognise your efforts.

The benefits

If you are only going to take away one benefit, it should be this: greater self-knowledge. More than just a professional asset, daring to look at yourself in the mirror and understanding how you work is a real advantage in life. The more you confront yourself, the more you will be able to correct your faults and make progress, because self-assessment is part of a process of continuous learning. Its other benefits include:

- the ability to analyse the situation and anticipate future difficulties;
- greater independence and versatility;
- a springboard to professional achievement.

A CLEARLY DEFINED GOAL

Although we may talk about "taking stock", this expression only really makes sense if something comes after it. Take stock of what? In what context? In order to know what direction to take, you must clarify your approach and define your aim as precisely as possible.

> ### **EXAMPLES**
>
> - I am currently an administrative worker, but in the next two years I want to start my own organic products company. What skills and knowledge do I need to succeed in my career change?
> - I am a project manager, and at the halfway stage of a project I would like to know where I am with it.
> - I want to get ready for one of the regular performances reviews at my company (in this case, your manager may require you to carry out self-assessment) by identifying what I bring to the business.

Be aware that you will not always set your goal yourself. If your manager asks you to "take stock of your involvement in the company", you can ask them to be more specific so that you know exactly what they expect from you.

When you have responsibility towards other people, it will sometimes be necessary to produce several grids for a single aim. As a project manager, for example, you will evaluate your work with regard to your company, but also to your client. Of course, these evaluations will not be developed in the same way.

THE RIGHT FRAME OF MIND

You should approach self-assessment with the right frame of mind, otherwise you may not carry it out correctly. Consequently, here are some principles to keep in mind.

Be positive

For many people, evaluation is unpleasant, because it is liable to lead to punishment. When your manager asks you to analyse a project which went badly, you sometimes adopt a defensive attitude out of fear that you will be blamed. You should keep in mind that the aim is to help you to make progress. If you encounter difficulties during the process, think about the benefits it will bring you. Admitting your faults and your mistakes can seem difficult, but naming them is the first step in your development.

Be objective

Emotion is the number one enemy of self-assessment, because our feelings can cloud our vision and harm our analysis. Furthermore, analysing ourselves clashes with our own self-esteem. As such, people with big egos risk overestimating themselves, while those with a low opinion of themselves will portray themselves negatively.

Consequently, this process requires you to be very objective, because in order to assess yourself you must base your evaluation on facts and not on opinions, such as "I think that my level is low" or "I don't think I do that well". Expressions like "it's good" and "it's bad" mean nothing in themselves: they only acquire meaning when they are linked to a concrete value, for example as part of a self-assessment grid.

Of course, there is no such thing as perfect objectivity, but that does not mean you cannot get close to it. Below are some tips to help you view your situation more objectively:

- Take on two personalities. Since it is easy to objectively judge someone else, imagine that you have been asked to analyse the situation of a colleague you do not know:

  > "I worked for several years with a colleague who had an original approach to preparing for his yearly review. He imagined that he was evaluating his twin rather than himself. For him, this was an ideal solution: by relying on the special bonds between him and his brother, he managed to gain a sense of perspective." (Jean-Claude, administrative associate in the public sector).

- Ask other people for their opinion on your work, your behaviour, etc.
- Get to know your own biases (meaning the distorted way each individual perceives reality) and, rather than trying to change them, compensate for them with strengths in your self-assessment grid.

Be realistic

Being objective will in particular help you to be more realistic, which is another essential principle. Indeed, for an effective self-assessment, you must find a middle ground and evaluate yourself pragmatically. Overestimating or underestimating yourself risks preventing you from achieving your goals. You may spend more time than you planned on tasks, refuse to ask for help as you are certain that you can cope by yourself, or turn down the chance to take part in a project out of fear that you will not be able to handle this extra work. In all these cases, demoralisation lies in wait. Do not try to ascribe false qualities or imaginary defects to yourself, as this will only harm you.

Be honest with yourself

When you have to answer to another person, you can look for excuses to try to get out of it; on the other hand, it will be much more difficult to lie to yourself, and burying your head in the sand will not get you anywhere. Face up to your responsibilities. Of course, sometimes there really are unforeseen circumstances, but most of the time failure is caused by a lack of willpower or discipline. Assessing yourself is extremely difficult because it makes you face up to your responsibilities, with no way out. Do not panic: nobody is asking you to get there straight away, but do not hide behind excuses!

THE SELF-ASSESSMENT GRID

This tool can help you to carry out your self-assessment. Structuring your thoughts and your skills in the form of a table lets you analyse them more easily. The assessment grid comprises three elements:

- **the criteria** are the elements which are assessed, and will allow you to judge the situation;
- **the observable elements** represent the behaviours or characteristics linked to the criteria;
- **the value scale** is the system for assessing your criteria. It is made up of levels which are assigned a value or a judgement.

Below is an example assessment grid. You will find other examples in the 'Over to you' section.

Am I a good project manager?

Criteria	Observable elements	Value scale (Levels)
Managing a team	• Motivating the team • Conflict resolution • Etc.	1 2 3 4 5 1 2 3 4 5
Managing a budget	• Evaluation of initial budget • Management of unforeseen circumstances • Etc.	1 2 3 4 5 1 2 3 4 5

Self-Assessment © 50MINUTES. com

EXTRA INFORMATION

The criteria and observable elements may differ depending on the degree of precision of your grid. In our example, the person is trying to get an overall view of their role as a manager with their strengths and weaknesses.

Once these have been identified, they could do another, more detailed analysis by looking at each criterion individually and assigning new observable elements to them. Whatever your situation, use precise elements to make the grid effective and determine whether you have reached your goals.

The evaluation criteria and observable elements

The choice of criteria is an essential step that you should pay maximum attention to, because your criteria must be relevant to the aim of the grid. If the self-assessment was requested by someone else, they must provide you with suitable criteria. You may therefore receive a ready-prepared grid. Nonetheless, it is generally up to you to determine these criteria with the help of your working documents, which describe your aims. For example, if you have been given specifications for the management of a project, you can judge yourself based on the objective, deadline, budget and resources set out in that document. Likewise, if you are going to your first performance review at a new job, you can base your assessment on the job description from the advert and on the objectives of your first tasks.

This choice is more difficult when you are working independently, because you have no superiors and you have to draw up your own criteria from nothing. Once again, the ideal approach is to take your objective as your starting point and describe it. You can organise your project based on different areas: communications, budget, team, etc. Whether or not you were the one who decided to carry out the self-assessment, keep these recommendations in mind:

- The criteria must be specific to your objective. If you are managing an international team, you could ask yourself whether you have managed to overcome cultural differences; this would obviously be meaningless in a national project. Some criteria are shared by multiple projects, but try to make them as specific as possible.
- Be precise and factual. If your self-assessment concerns a particular phase of a project, indicate this period clearly and only take into account the events which relate to it.
- Gather information. You can consult the accounts of people who have experienced similar situations, get in touch with associations which are active in your sector, or look for models on the internet. This approach will allow you to find elements that you might not have thought of. Furthermore, comparing your sources will allow you to identify the most commonly cited criteria and those that are hardly mentioned: this could be a good indicator of their relevance.

For each criterion listed, ask yourself how it is indispensable for achieving the objective set. The more specific they are, the clearer your idea of the situation will be! Depending on the situation, however, you do not always need to explain everything in detail. In fact, the grid can give you a general overview (if you are at the start of a project) in order to prepare the groundwork or look at things in more depth. Furthermore, you should make sure that the information does not overlap: your observable elements cannot belong to more than one criterion. If this is the case, make your

criteria more specific. There are two methods of drawing up
your criteria:

- list all the observable elements, then group them by
  categories. These will form the different criteria;
- define the criteria first of all and then look for the corres-
  ponding observable elements.

If your grid focuses on a situation that you do not know well
(for example, a career change), opt for the second method;
otherwise, choose depending on your preference. Whatever
method you use, try not to have more than ten criteria so as
not to spread yourself too thin. The criteria can be expressed
in the following forms:

- questions: "Was I able to motivate my team?";
- statements: "I am able to motivate my team";
- actions or skills: "Ability to motivate my team".

The value scale

We can distinguish two types of scales: scales whose levels
have a value and scales whose levels are judgements.

The first category comprises numerical scales (1, 2, 3, 4, 5)
and alphabetical scales (A, B, C, D, E). If you prefer a visual
medium, you can also opt for a graphic representation. In
the second category, the scales have a qualitative value such
as 'poor', 'fair', 'good', 'very good', 'excellent'. You can also
use a symbolic representation (emoticons, meteorological
concepts, etc.) to add some life to your table.

Recap table

Scale	Type of scale	Usefulness
1 2 3 4 5	Numerical scale	The most classic scale, ideal for self-assessment. It allows several grids to be compared easily, if you put a programme in place.
A B C D E	Alphabetical scale	See above
	Graphical scale	Its advantages are aesthetic rather than practical. Do not try to be too precise, or you risk spending a lot of unnecessary time on it. Conversely, if you complete it by eye, it will be too imprecise. A tip: divide it into five or ten portions to make it more visual.
Unacceptable, fair, satisfactory, good, excellent	Qualitative scale	Its major asset is that it is adjustable: you can formulate different scales depending on the criteria.
☹ 😐 ☺	Symbolic scale	This scale make the assessment feel less school-like and makes it look more pleasant.

<u>Some tips</u>

- There are normally between three and seven levels so as to stop the exercise from becoming too complicated. Two levels are often used for the values 'yes' and 'no'. You should also opt for

an odd number as this allows you to identify the median. In many cases, five is the ideal number.
- The scales are usually in ascending order: the lowest value is on the left and the highest on the right.
- Whatever scale you choose, you should precisely define what each level means. In a scale with five levels, does the third mean 3/5 (60%), or does it signify half (50%)? And in both cases, how do you decide whether or not a rating has been achieved?

Analysing your responses

Once you have filled in your grid, identify the criteria which stand out as positive and the criteria which are negative in order to find out which skills you have already acquired and which you need to improve. You can work out your average rating to obtain an overall view of the situation. However, you should balance out your judgement, because the criteria do not necessarily all have the same weight. You can classify them as priority and secondary elements. As such, if you have poor results for your secondary criteria but very good results for your priority criteria, you are closer to your goal than the other way around.

It is now time to ask yourself about the reasons and factors which explain these results, in order to avoid repeating the same mistakes. Your situation will influence the type of explanations you look for.

- If it is a professional project, there could be unforeseen circumstances that are outside your control (illness, bankruptcy of a partner company in the project, etc.). Nonetheless, be careful not to offload all responsibility: if you have gone over budget or missed the deadline, you may not have estimated them correctly. If your team has not reached its goal, you could have communicated it poorly to the team members.

- If you are preparing for a yearly performance review, you might realise that you have not been able to complete the necessary quota of work. Did you work too slowly? If this is the case, why are you losing time? Were you disturbed by a colleague? Is it the first time you have done this kind of task?

The analysis of each self-assessment depends in part on the situation and the objective. Once you have determined your areas for improvement and the skills you have mastered, you can make use of this information to look for solutions and to progress: undertake training, gather information about a particular subject, draw up a procedure to avoid making the same mistakes again, organise a meeting to refocus the team, etc.

THE SELF-ASSESSMENT PROGRAMME

For many people, self-assessment is limited to an occasional appraisal: they draw up their grid, fill it out, draw their conclusions and move on to something else! However, the process does not stop there. When you have found suitable solutions to achieve your goal, you should make sure that you follow through on them. To do this, establish an assessment programme by planning appraisals at the beginning and at the end, but also during the process. These intermediary appraisals could be set up:

- At regular intervals (every week, fortnight, month, quarter, half-year) depending on the length of your programme. Of course, if you run into particular difficulties, do not wait for the next self-assessment, but rethink your tactics as soon as possible.
- When you have achieved an intermediary goal (acquired a new skill, achieved a sub-objective of the project, etc.).

You must pay particular attention to the initial appraisal, which will be a starting point for drawing up the outline of your project, and to the final appraisal, which closes the project and allows you to draw conclusions that will benefit you in future tasks. Setting up a self-assessment programme will allow you to:

- be more independent;
- alter your path towards your goals;

- progress at your own pace.

Extra information

A self-assessment programme can prove useful in any kind of job. By evaluating yourself regularly, you will be able to improve your efficiency and identify any declines in momentum. Furthermore, you will arrive at your performance review better prepared, because you will have real arguments to back up your points.

TOP TIPS

- To ensure that your self-assessment is constructive, take care to carry it out in good conditions. Settle down somewhere calm, in a place and at a time when you will not be disturbed. You should also be in the right frame of mind: relaxed, unstressed and ready to reason positively. Finally, do not rush and take time to think over each criterion.

- Be as objective as possible. Inventing skills that you do not really have will not help you to improve; on the contrary, you could fail to achieve your aim or lose credibility with your employer. The goal of self-assessment is to correctly gauge your own worth, to highlight your good qualities and to reassess your weak points.

- Before starting to draw up your grid, think about what suits you best: what form? What value scale and what representation? Feel free to create your own notation system, but do not forget to give each level a precise value. You should devote as much attention to the creation of your grid as to your responses.

- In some situations, it can be useful to assess your knowledge of a criterion independently of your ability to put it into practice (know-how). Draw up two grids and compare them!

- Feel free to draw up multiple grids: in some cases, the object of your assessment covers a range of themes, which it would be too complicated to put in a single grid. Think back to the example of the administrative worker who wants to launch their own range of organic products:

they should draw up a grid for entrepreneurship skills, a grid to check how much they know about the organic products market, etc.

- Compare your results to those of your previous assessments but also, if possible, to those of your colleagues. This little competition should have a positive goal: helping yourself improve by taking the best elements of each assessment.
- Attach importance to your self-esteem. This is linked to the judgement that you make about yourself. When a person's self-esteem is low, they tend to give themselves poor ratings, to not notice progress, and even to sabotage their own success. A self-assessment grid aims to stop your self-confidence from interfering in the appraisal of your skills (both positively and negatively), even if complete objectivity seems almost impossible. Try to understand how you see yourself. Some disciplines, such as yoga and meditation, can help you with this.
- Find an appropriate way of celebrating each goal reached and each self-assessment completed, and associate them with a reward. If you end up with negative results, shift your perspective to turn them into something positive: view them as a new challenge and think about your future success!
- Display your grid somewhere visible and look at it regularly: you will then pay more attention to your past weaknesses.

FAQS

WHEN SHOULD I ASSESS MYSELF?

In any personal or professional situation (launch of a new project, change of position, career change); anything can be evaluated! We could spend our whole lives analysing our actions, but this would be very tedious. Self-assessment is therefore particularly recommended before making an important decision, because it will enable us to get a good grasp of the issues and risks at play and to choose the right path. For that reason, it should be an integral part of all individual or collective projects.

It also seems useful to carry out an appraisal when we feel that something is not working, whether in our private or professional life, in order to change course in time. However, the ideal approach is to plan assessment sessions regularly so as to anticipate these situations. Do not see self-assessment as a chore, but remain one step ahead of it and make it your greatest asset.

HOW OFTEN SHOULD I PLAN SELF-ASSESSMENT SESSIONS?

Opt for a weekly assessment session of between half an hour and an hour. Friday is a good choice, because then you can evaluate the week that has just gone and plan the next week. With regard to the ideal time to carry out the assessment, there are a number of possibilities:

- Right at the start of the day, between 8 am and 10 am: you are still fresh and in great shape to tackle this phase of intense work.
- Conversely, you could do it at the end of the afternoon (between 3 pm and 5 pm, for example). At that time, you will be in the opposite situation: you are looking towards the weekend and you are not in the mood for your day-to-day work. You can leave it and move onto another task with your self-assessment. This choice is based on psychology: like a film or a novel which throws all its energy into its ending, you are concentrating one last time and you put everything into your personal assessment. However, the timing means that there is a greater risk of rushing the exercise.

If you work on medium-term (several months) and long-term (a year or more) projects, leave more space between your assessments, but do not hesitate to do one if a doubt or a problem emerges. Imagine how much time you would have wasted if you found out after a month that you were on the wrong track! You should also think about carrying out an evaluation each time you achieve one of your sub-objectives. These different assessments will allow you to observe your progress and identify areas for improvement.

WHAT DANGERS AM I LIKELY TO ENCOUNTER WHEN I ASSESS MYSELF?

The greatest danger is you! It is tempting to embellish your assessment. This satisfies your ego, but it can harm you over the long term, and above all it makes the process useless.

You should be honest and objective with yourself in order to draw realistic conclusions.

Drawing up a self-assessment grid can also be arduous. Sometimes, you must produce it using criteria that you do not know or that you do not have a good grasp of. Depending on your situation, gather information from associations and organisations that could help you.

WHAT IS THE DIFFERENCE BETWEEN AN ASSESSMENT GRID AND A SELF-ASSESSMENT GRID?

They differ in that the former is carried out with the aim of determining someone else's skills, while the latter is drawn up for a person to evaluate themselves. This has consequences, particularly regarding the choice of criteria to consider or the value scale used. For example, the levels of an assessment grid must be explicit enough for all users to interpret it in the same way, at the risk of distorting the results. This is why descriptive levels (fair, satisfactory, etc.) are preferred in education.

HOW CAN SELF-ASSESSMENT HELP ME TO PREPARE FOR MY YEARLY PERFORMANCE REVIEW?

In business, employees regularly undergo evaluations which use various methodologies: filling in questionnaires, writing reports, etc. Sometimes, you will also be asked to assess yourself; this will then be compared with your manager's opinion. However, we are often underprepared for this exercise and our appraisals often prove to be incomplete. Indeed, it is difficult to remember project X which was finalised three months ago if we did not take notes! By establishing your own programme of self-assessment, you can also regularly evaluate your work and keep a written record of it. Even if this exercise is entirely unofficial, it will benefit you because you will be ready to carry out a critical appraisal of your work when you meet with your manager.

WHAT SHOULD I DO IF THE RESULTS OF MY PERSONAL ASSESSMENT ARE DIFFERENT FROM MY YEARLY PERFORMANCE REVIEW?

Start by asking yourself why your manager views your work differently. Know that it is not necessarily the case that one of you is right and the other is wrong: this difference could be due to information that is not known by one or both parties. Check that you are basing your assessment on all the facts and not on opinions or hearsay. Maybe you think that the evaluation criteria are unfair. In that case, explain your point of view. If your comments are relevant, you will probably score points.

If your manager is clearly wrong, the situation is trickier. However, you can still try to put forward arguments without being accusatory or aggressive towards them. If you have prepared for the review well, you should be able to answer all their questions. Conversely, if you are the one who is in the wrong, do not try to deny it, but pick yourself up and offer solutions. Afterwards, you can go back to your self-assessment to understand where you went wrong.

SHOULD I ENCOURAGE MY EMPLOYEES TO ASSESS THEMSELVES?

Absolutely! You will make them more independent and more aware of their responsibilities. Self-assessment is so effective that, according to the *Business Insider* article "This is the Internal Grading System Google Uses for Its Employees – And You Should Use It Too", Google made it part of its work from its first years onwards. For each goal set (determined by the employees themselves), Google teams rated themselves rather than being judged by their manager. Google uses scoring of between 0 and 1, with the aim being to get 0.6 or 0.7. If you are close to 1, that means that the goal is not ambitious enough. Conversely, a team with a score of below 0.4 should ask itself questions about its work.

OVER TO YOU

It would not be much of an exaggeration to say that there are almost as many grids as there are users and situations! In order to carry out effective self-assessment, you should draw up your grid beforehand. Use the following examples for inspiration.

THE CLASSIC GRID

Title of your grid

Criteria	Observable elements	Value scale (Levels)					Comments
Criterion 1	• Observable element 1	1	2	3	4	5	
	• Observable element 2	1	2	3	4	5	
	• Etc.	1	2	3	4	5	
Criterion 2	• Observable element 1	1	2	3	4	5	
	• Observable element 2	1	2	3	4	5	
	• Etc.	1	2	3	4	5	

This type of grid has proven its worth and remains effective. You can use the 'Comments' box to describe the situation you have experienced or justify your evaluation of it. However, to avoid making the sheet too full, keep to a short comment (maximum three lines) or even just to some key words. Finally, for a better spaced presentation, draw up your grid in landscape format.

THE BINARY SCALE GRID

Formulate criteria in the form of questions or statements, answer "yes" or "no" and explain your choice. This model forces you to decide one way or the other, which is both its strength and its weakness. It emphasises the why, rather than the answer itself, and in this way allows you to better understand what is holding you back.

The binary scale grid

Criteria	Yes-No	Explanation
Did I communicate all the necessary information to my team?	No	After a week, I realised that my team was contacting suppliers when a market study was already underway.

THE SEMI-OPEN GRID

This grid includes some open questions. It is often used to give feedback (on a training course, for example) or during annual performance reviews. It allows the majority of responses to be targeted, while leaving the user a margin of discretion. As part of a self-assessment session, you can include some open questions in order to broaden your outlook.

To go back to the example above, we could imagine the open question: "Is this a unique situation in my company, or have there been similar cases? What happened then?"

The semi-open grid

	Criteria	Scale				
	Criteria	**Scale**				
Closed assessment	Organisation	1	2	3	4	5
	Time management	1	2	3	4	5
	Management of financial resources	1	2	3	4	5
	Management of material resources	1	2	3	4	5
	Criteria					
Open assessment	What were my strong points in the management of this project? Response					
	What were my weak points in the management of this project? Response					

FURTHER READING

BILBIOGRAPHY

- Debray, C. and Famery, S. (2010) *Le bilan de compétences.* Paris: Éditions d'Organisation.
- Korenblit, P., Lehongre, H and Nicolas, C. (2011) *Construire son projet professionnel... à partir du bilan de compétences.* Paris: ESF éditeur.
- Labruffe, A. (2009) *Les nouveaux outils de l'évaluation des compétences.* Paris: AFNOR Éditions.
- Batime, C. and Bonvalot, G. (2003) *Penser avec l'entraî-nement mental. Agir dans la complexité.* Lyon: Chronique sociale.
- Yarrow, J. (2014) This Is The Internal Grading System Google Uses For Its Employees – And You Should Use It Too. *Business Insider.* [Online]. [Accessed 9 November 2016]. Available from: <http://www.businessinsider.com/googles-ranking-system-okr-2014-1?IR=T>
- Yatchinovsky, A. and Michard, P. (1994) Le *bilan personnel et professionnel. Instrument de management.* Paris: ESF éditeur.

ADDITIONAL SOURCES

Skills appraisal and career development

- Cottrell, S. (2003) *Skills for Success: The Personal Development Planning Handbook.* Basingstoke: Palgrave Macmillan.

- Harrington, B. and Hall, B. T. (2007) *Career Management & Work-Life Integration: Using Self-Assessment to Navigate Contemporary Careers*. California: Sage Publications, Inc.
- Yates, J. (2013) *The Career Coaching Handbook*. Abingdon: Routledge.

Independent learning and self-knowledge

- Haward, T. (2007) The *Practical Guide to Independent Learning Skills*. London: Network Continuum Education.
- Neff, G. and Nafus, D. (2016) *Self-tracking*. Cambridge, Massachusetts: Massachusetts Institute of Technology.

Performance reviews

- Armstrong, S. (2010) *Essential Performance Review Handbook: A Quick and Handy Resource for Any Manager or HR Professional*. New Jersey: Career Press.
- Harvard Business Review (2015) *Performance Reviews*. Boston: Harvard Business School Press.
- Kessler, R. (2008) *Competency-Based Performance Reviews: How to Perform Employee Evaluations the Fortune 500 Way*. New Jersey: Career Press.

50MINUTES.com

IMPROVE YOUR GENERAL KNOWLEDGE
IN A BLINK OF AN EYE !

www.50minutes.com